# ONCE UPON A TIME NOT SO LONG AGO

JENNIFER GRANT

ILLUSTRATED BY GILLIAN WHITING

 Morehouse Publishing
NEW YORK

Church Publishing Incorporated
19 East 34th Street
New York, NY 10016

Cover design by: Jennifer Kopec, 2Pug Design
Typeset by: Progressive Publishing Services

A record of this book is available from the Library of Congress.

ISBN-13: 9781640654037 (hardcover)
ISBN-13: 9781640654044 (ebook)

Printed in Canada.

For Evelyn and Emmaline with love.

- JG

For my Mom, there isn't a day
I don't miss you or a day
I don't see the joy you left behind.

- GW

Given with love from

_____

to

_____

on this date _____

Once upon a time
not so long ago,
a lot of people,
all over the world,
got sick.

The ones who *weren't* sick worried about getting sick.

Most people had to stay home,
but some people had to go to work.

Many people died.

It was a very hard time . . .

but not everything was bad.

The city was so quiet you could hear
the birds sing.

Dogs were happy because their
people stayed home with them.

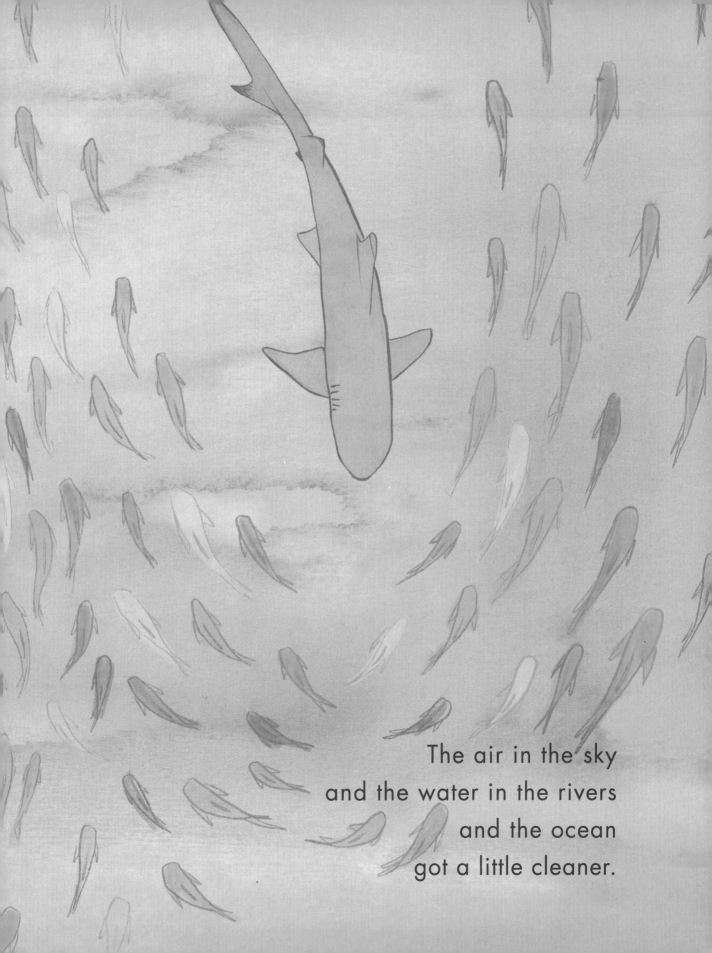

The air in the sky
and the water in the rivers
and the ocean
got a little cleaner.

Some people planted seeds
and waited for them to sprout

and peek up through the dirt.

People learned to do
things in new ways.

Many, many people were kind.

Then, finally,
        things started getting better.

People started going to school
and work again,
and they could pray in churches
and temples again,
and laugh together again,
all in the same room.

But things were different from the beforetimes . . .
people had changed.

They went outside more than they
did before the sickness came,
and they spent more time looking
up at the sky, too.

The people had learned something:

Now they knew that the most important things
aren't *things* at all.

Once upon a time not so long ago,
we went through a very hard time,
and we learned how wonderful it is
to be together and to hold each other close.

What will you remember most
about these times?

What or who did you miss most?

What good things happened
during these days?